Everything You Need to Know About

LIVING WITH YOUR BABY AND YOUR PARENTS UNDER ONE ROOF

There are advantages and disadvantages to raising your baby in your parents' home.

Everything You Need to Know About

LIVING WITH YOUR BABY AND YOUR PARENTS UNDER ONE ROOF

Carolyn Simpson

THE ROSEN PUBLISHING GROUP, INC.
NEW YORK

Published in 1996, 1998 by The Rosen Publishing Group, Inc.
29 East 21st Street, New York, NY 10010

Copyright © 1996, 1998 by The Rosen Publishing Group, Inc.

Revised Edition 1998

Library of Congress Cataloging-in-Publication Data

Simpson, Carolyn.
   Everything you need to know about living with your baby and your parents under one roof / Carolyn Simpson
        p.   cm. — (The need to know library)
   Includes bibliographical references and index.
   Summary: A guide for all teenage parents trying to raise their babies while living at home with their own parents.
   ISBN 0-8239-2840-3
   1. Teenage parents—Lifeskills guides. [1. Teenage parents. 2. Parenting.] I. Series.
HQ759.64.S56 1995
646.7'00835   95-8762
                                                                                        CIP
                                                                                         AC

Manufactured in the United States of America

Contents

Introduction

This book is for teenagers who are becoming parents. One-third of teenage mothers quit high school. Without important job skills, they have trouble getting and keeping good jobs. Teenage dads who care for their children face the same problems. And it's always hard work to raise a child.

How can teen parents take care of themselves and their babies? Some teenage parents decide to stay in their parents' homes.

This book will help you decide whether to live at home with your baby. If you live with your parents, it will help everyone get along together.

Michael and Shawna hadn't planned to have a baby. One night they had sex without a condom. They thought nothing would happen.

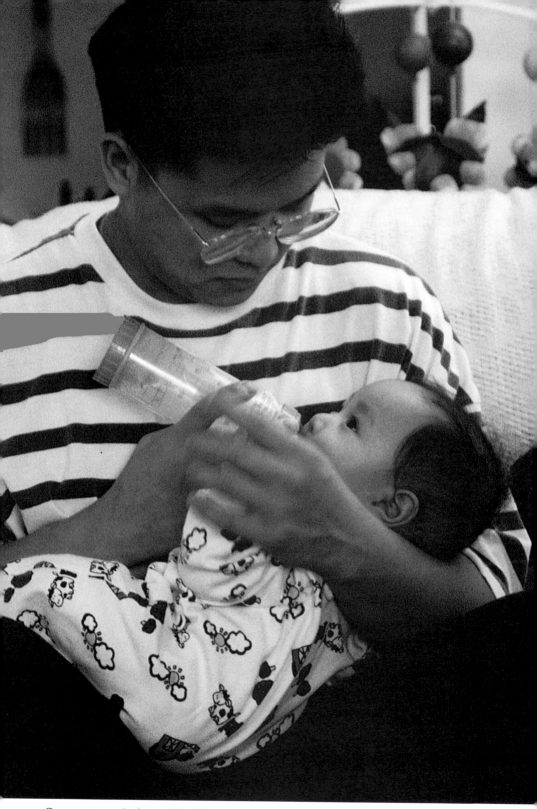

Some teen fathers decide to raise their babies themselves.

But it did happen. When Shawna missed her period for two months, she went to the doctor. She was pregnant.

"What are we going to do?" Shawna asked Michael. "I don't want an abortion. And I don't want strangers raising my child." Shawna started to cry.

Michael took Shawna in his arms. "I don't know," he answered. "I love you, but I haven't finished high school. How can I earn enough money to care for three people?"

Michael sounded scared. Shawna was scared, too. What if he left her? She didn't know anything about child care. She didn't have money for a place of her own. And she couldn't work or go to school if she had to care for a baby alone.

"Maybe we can live with our parents," Michael said. "Let's tell them what happened."

Most parents are upset when they learn that their children are sexually active. The boy's parents may blame the girl. The girl's parents may dislike the baby's father.

Parents also know that it's hard work to raise a child. And it's important work because it involves a human being. They aren't always eager to start over.

Shawna and Michael went together to see Shawna's mom. She was angry. She had told Shawna not to have sex until she was married.

"I can't help you," Shawna's mom said. "What

would I do with the baby while I work at the school cafeteria? Besides, I've got two other kids of my own. I don't want to raise yours, too!"

Michael's mom and dad were upset, too. They wanted Michael to go to college. He was their youngest son. They didn't want to raise more kids.

Most parents need time to adjust. Give them time to think about what's happening. They may be willing to help after all. They may even feel proud that you're facing your situation.

Later, Shawna's and Michael's parents agreed to meet with the young couple.

"Sometimes I can baby-sit at my house at night," Shawna's mother said. *"Or maybe on weekends, when Shawna and Michael have jobs. I'll buy the baby's formula, too."*

"Michael and Shawna and their baby can live with us for a while," Michael's mom volunteered. *"I'll baby-sit while they go to school. But they'll need to help me, too. It will take lots of planning to make things work."*

Eighty-two percent of welfare mothers fifteen to seventeen years old live with relatives for at least a year after their children are born. This book covers three possibilities: the couple raising the baby while living with one set of parents; the father raising the baby while living with his parents; and the mother raising the baby while living with her parents.

One situation is not always better than another. Some couples marry; some don't. Some fathers stay in touch; some don't. Some mothers end up living with the boyfriend's parents. What seems to matter most is having the support of parents.

So how do you decide that living with your baby and your parents is the right choice? It's the right choice if you (the baby's mother and/or father) cannot support yourselves but have a good relationship with parents who can help support you. You aren't saying you'll live with them forever.

Legal Issues

Who ought to raise the baby? Ideally, both parents (married or not) should have a hand in it. Legally, both of you are responsible for your baby's financial needs until he or she is eighteen years old. Even if you break up (or the father wants nothing to do with you both), *by law* you're both expected to provide child support.

Laws do vary from state to state. If you (the baby's mother) are worried about putting the baby's father's name on the birth certificate (because you don't want him visiting), you should talk with a lawyer in your area. The father still exists (with rights and all) even if you don't specifically name him.

If you (the baby's father) believe you can strike a deal with the baby's mother to avoid child-support payments, consult a lawyer, too. In almost every case, the baby's parents have both the right to visit the child and the responsibility to support the child unless the court says otherwise. The two of you cannot negotiate those matters yourselves.

And lastly, if you (the baby's father) want to raise the baby yourself, you should check with a lawyer. In many states you can file for custody of your baby if you think your baby's mother is neglecting him or her. Then the courts will step in and check it out.

If you can't afford a lawyer, call your county Legal Aid Society or courthouse. They'll help you get free or inexpensive legal advice.

Married or not, if you continue to see each other, you'll have many responsibilities to work out. Not just with each other, but with your parents as well.

That's where this book can help.

Although it may be difficult while you both live in the same house with your parents, it is important to spend time alone as a couple to maintain a healthy relationship.

Chapter 1

Choosing Where to Live

You're about to have your baby. Will you and your child live with your parents? If so, how will everyone fit comfortably in the house? You have important decisions to make.

The Couple

Let's assume that the baby's mother and the baby's father decide to live together and raise their child. You need to learn how to care for a baby, but you have a few other problems, too. For example, where will you live? And should you get married?

Many teenagers can't afford to live on their own, even if they are married. Sometimes it makes more sense to start off living with one set of parents. If you married with family approval, you can probably choose which parents to live with. But think about:

- Which family has more room?
- Which family is more willing to have an infant in the home?
- Which family gets along best with the teenager who'll be home the most?

If you go to school or work, you'll probably have to pay between $52 and $70 a week for child care.

If you as a couple don't get married, you may have fewer choices. You may have to live with the parents who don't mind your living together.

Okay. You have a home and parents who are willing to help. But what about "personal space"? How exactly are you all going to fit?

If you were lucky enough to have had your own bedroom, you may be able to fit in two more people. If you didn't have your own room, or it's too small, think about making a room in the attic or basement. It doesn't have to be a palace—just a place to give you some privacy.

Make sure you can close a door on the rest of the household. As a couple, you are sure to want privacy and time to be alone with each other. As a family, you may want time alone, too. And it will help insulate the rest of the house if your baby cries for long periods during the night.

When you're living with your parents, it's sometimes difficult to decide how much of your problems you should share with them, at least about your relationship. If you choose to tell them all about

Living together can introduce new tensions into a relationship.

every fight you and your boyfriend/husband have, you will upset the household. You two may make up soon enough, but your parents may be upset a lot longer. Also there are certain areas of your life that they don't need to hear about—like your sex life. (You don't want to hear about theirs, do you?)

Living with your partner can be a very difficult, stressful experience. At best, you may discover that you are wonderfully compatible. At worst, you may find that your partner is not a person with whom you can have a healthy relationship; he or she may even be abusive. If you're being hurt, get help fast. Tell your parents or a reliable neighbor. Call 911 or a domestic violence hotline (listed in the front of the phone book). Don't assume that your partner will change just because he's sorry later. People who abuse others rarely stop without outside help. If he starts hurting you, how long before he'll start hurting the baby?

The Father

You've decided to raise your baby with your parents' help. You may want to put the baby in the same room as the person who'll be caring for it most of the time. That's just a convenience. If you'll be working nights and going to school during the day, your mom may want the baby closer to her. Of course, if you're going to be the caregiver through the night, you'll want the baby in your room.

Babies tend to disrupt a household. If your father or mother works outside the home, you will have to do much more of the baby care. Not only that, your parents may be disturbed by the baby's crying at night. You may want to move your room to a different part of the house. Raising your own baby as a teen father is an untraditional move, and you'll need all the support you can get. Be sure to save some private time for yourself. You can still have dreams and goals.

The Mother

As a rule, more teen mothers raise their kids

You may need to share your space with your baby.

than do couples. Even so, you need to carve out
some personal space for the baby and yourself.
Siblings should not have to share their bedroom
with your infant. If you don't have your own room,
see if your parents can make a special place for
you in the attic, basement, or a spare room. You
need to be close to them, but you want your
privacy all the same. Shannon, a young woman I
know, shared her bedroom with her twin boys.
The room looked more like a day-care center than
a teenager's bedroom. Her parents squeezed two
little cribs on either side of her own small bed.
Shannon's chest of drawers now held more baby
clothes than jeans, T-shirts, and socks. And
though she was a good mother and loved her

little boys, there were times Shannon wished she could close her bedroom door and be alone.

Babies turn households upside down. Jars of baby food fill the kitchen cabinets, used baby bottles fill the sink, and cans of formula take over the countertops. When you live with your parents, try not to let your baby's food, toys, and clothes take over the house. Agree with your folks on which cupboards will hold the baby stuff, and stick to that.

Personal Space

Something you'll all need—parents, teen couple, or single new parent—is time alone. Just as you'll want privacy, provide the same for your parents. Take an afternoon stroll with the baby, or go out for an evening with the baby to a friend's house. Give your Mom and Dad some time to themselves. They'll need it too. After all, how many years have they already been parents?

Chapter 2

Household Chores and Expenses

*A*rmando was glad his mom let him live at home with his baby. At first things seemed to go okay. Armando's mom baby-sat while he went to school. When Armando was home, the baby took lots of his time. He was always tired, so he slept while the baby napped. Sometimes his sister baby-sat so he could be with friends.

Then Armando and his mother began having trouble getting along. His mother complained that Armando didn't help with the cleaning or washing. He left baby bottles in the sink and smelly diapers in the bathroom. Armando's mom refused to baby-sit anymore.

Armando realized he'd have to take on more household jobs. He wanted to get along with his mom.

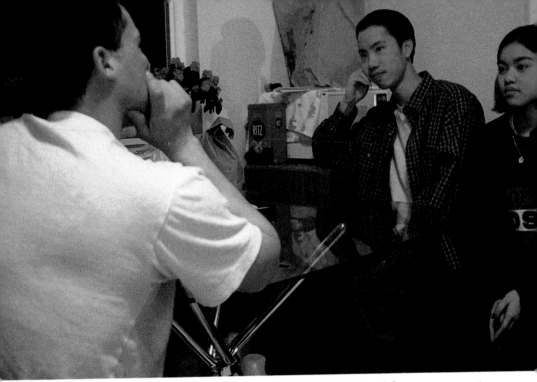

The first thing you have to do is sit down with your parents and decide who is responsible for what.

The Couple

Usually the couple end up living with the parents that are the most supportive. But problems still can crop up. What if you, the teenage mother, live with your boyfriend/ husband's parents? Maybe you're not too comfortable around his folks. How do you decide who does the dishes, prepares the meals, cleans the house, not to mention taking care of the baby?

First, you all need to sit down and discuss who takes care of what in the house. Most of the time, it depends on whether the parents work outside the home, whether the teen parents work or go to school, and whether the parents *want* the younger parents helping out.

Ask your parents or in-laws what your jobs can be. If you expect to be living there for a while, you'll feel better sharing the chores.

If you want to be treated as an adult, you have to act like one. And doing chores is part of being an adult. (Not exactly the fun part, of course . . .)

Here's a sample division of chores:

Baby's grandmother (who works outside the home)

> prepares menus (perhaps with baby's mother's help)
>
> does regular household chores: cleaning, dusting
>
> does family laundry
>
> cooks on weekends, makes breakfasts daily
>
> cleans up dishes on weeknights
>
> helps out with baby-sitting when arranged ahead of time
>
> grocery-shops

Baby's mother

> attends school with baby (who goes to day care)
>
> keeps room clean/picks up baby toys
>
> vacuums house twice weekly
>
> tends to baby when home (feeds baby, changes diaper)
>
> does couple's and baby's laundry
>
> prepares dinner, according to menus
>
> takes baby to doctor appointments
>
> takes turns tending to baby at night

School, working part time, and parenting can be exhausting.

Baby's father
    goes to school
    tends to baby when home (feeds baby, changes
        diaper)
    takes turns tending to baby at night
    helps with grocery-shopping
    does yard chores/helps with maintenance on car
    holds down at least a part-time job

Here's another sample:
Baby's grandmother (who cares for baby at home)
    tends to baby during school hours (feeding,
        changing, putting down for naps)
    prepares meals
    does family laundry
    does household cleaning

takes baby to doctor appointments (with baby's
mother, if possible)

Baby's mother

attends school

vacuums twice a week, or more often as needed

does own laundry (including baby's)

keeps room clean, picks up baby toys

helps out with dinner and cleanup

tends to baby through evening and night (feeding,
changing diaper, putting to bed)

You don't have to follow this exact list. Perhaps one
of you prefers doing dishes to cooking. The important
thing is to decide the chores ahead of time and follow
a plan. Once you've decided, write the job list down
on paper and have everyone concerned sign the paper.
That makes it a contract, and in the future, no one can
claim a job wasn't his or her responsibility. It'll be
there in black and white.

And, speaking of expenses, here's a short list of
things that teenage parents will need to cover.

diapers (anywhere from $10 to $15 a week)

wipes ($2 a week)

formula/food ($25 to $30)

well-baby exams by doctor (with HMO: maybe
$10/visit or $2.50/week

baby powder, soap, shampoo, laundry soap ($5 a
week)

medical insurance payments, prescriptions, child-
care, emergency doctor visits as needed

room and board (as agreed upon with your parents)
clothing needs; initially:

T-shirts

sleepers

blankets

crib bedding

jacket

one-piece outfits

sweaters

warm hat in winter and
sun hat in summer

bibs

pacifiers, bottles, teething rings and toys
baby items: stroller, high chair, car seat and crib
that meet current federal safety requirements

The Father

You may not have much time for chores if you're
raising a baby, going to school, and holding down a
job. Your part may be relieving your mother of child-
care duties when you're home. If you work, you could
help out with household expenses, because they'll cer-
tainly go up with a baby in the house.

Maybe you can't do the dishes or mow the lawn regularly, but you can buy diapers and formula. If you use
the family car, pay for the gas. If you buy a car (especially if your parents cosign the bank note), make your
payments on time and take out insurance coverage.

You'll feel better about the help you receive if you're
helping out, too.

It is important for you to contribute to the raising of your baby.

The Mother

Often, teenage mothers live with their own parents. But sometimes they are overwhelmed with all the new responsibilities. They are physically tired from pregnancy and giving birth, and they feel let down once the newness wears off. (Babies often seem to behave better in the hospital than they do when you get them home.) New mothers want to be babied too. So at first you may not feel like doing *any* chores. Just feeding the baby seems enough of a job.

But it's not fair to expect your parents to baby both you and their grandchild for long. If you want to be treated as an adult, you have to share in the responsibilities: helping out with meals, cleaning, and child care. Your parents didn't sign on to be parents again; *you* did.

If your parents can't afford to help you feed and clothe your baby, you can get help from welfare assistance. Diapers cost a lot of money. So does formula, if you don't breast-feed. And neither can be skimped on. You can't reuse paper diapers, and if you stretch formula with extra water you endanger your baby's health. These are expenses you have to meet.

Sharing responsibilities shows maturity. It tells your parents that you are competent. And don't complain while you do your fair share.

Chapter 3

Child Care and Discipline

*P*amela *was 16 when she had her first baby.*
Her parents said they would help her so she could
finish school. Pamela's mother stayed home all day
and took care of the baby. Pamela went to school;
then she'd go over to a friend's house. Most weekends
she went out on dates.

Baby Lisa saw more of her grandmother than of
her mother. So it was no surprise when she started
calling Pamela's mother "Mama" instead of
"Grandma." She even called Pamela "Pammie"
because that was what Pam's mother called her.

Pamela hadn't minded when her mother had done
the diapering and feeding in the middle of the night.
But when Lisa became more active, Pamela became
more interested. Lisa wouldn't call her "Mama,"
though, and Pamela was hurt.

The point of the story is clear: If you want to be
the parent, you must take responsibility—even for
the dirty jobs.

As a parent, you, not your parents, are responsible for all aspects of caring for your child or children.

The Couple

As a couple, you are more apt to lean on each other for support. You don't have to rely on your parents to get up for night feedings. You have each other.

You can ask your parents for advice. You can work out an arrangement for them to take care of your baby for short periods of time. But if you two want to be the parents, you have to do most of the child care.

First, you need to talk over your respective responsibilities:

- Will one of you stay home to tend the baby?
- Will one of you work to help with baby expenses?
- Which one will get up at night to feed the baby, or will you trade off nights?
- Which one will shop for the baby?
- Babies don't need disciplining, but toddlers do. How will you handle it?

Next, you have to decide how much help you want from your parents—and, of course, talk with them about how much they want to give:

- Do you need them to baby-sit during the day?
- Do you need their help to buy diapers and formula?
- Do you need them to take the baby to the doctor for checkups?

- Do you just want their advice?
- Do you all agree on the discipline: Is spanking okay? If so, who can do the spanking and for what reason? Should you set limits? Scold the child? Make time-outs?

When you've all agreed on your roles, things should go smoothly, and your baby will know Mom and Dad.

Different Childrearing Philosophies

You and your baby's other parent grew up in different homes. You may not agree on child-rearing methods. And the baby's grandparents raised you. They may want to use their methods on your child.

It's best if everyone who cares for your baby agrees on methods of discipline. Different approaches may confuse a baby and make him feel insecure.

The parents who care for the baby must decide how to deal with certain situations. Get advice from other parents you admire. Read books and articles about discipline. Then explain to everyone who cares for your baby how you want certain situations handled.

For example, will you pick up the baby whenever he cries? Comforting a fussy baby takes lots of time and energy. Of course, you'll always check to be sure the baby is not hungry or wet or in pain. If he's okay, he may need to fuss a little to get back to sleep. However, picking up a baby doesn't spoil him. If you comfort your child when he's upset, he'll learn to trust. He'll feel safe and loved.

What if he just won't stop crying? You may feel really angry and helpless. If a baby's crying gets to you, ask someone to help you quiet him. Or put him in his crib, where he'll be safe. Go into another room where his crying won't bother you so much, and check him often to make sure he's okay. Never, never hit or shake a baby. Everyone must agree on this. Hitting or shaking a baby can kill him. Or it can hurt his brain permanently.

Decide how you'll handle the baby when he becomes a toddler and can walk (and run!) around. At first your child doesn't know good behavior from bad. He just wants to explore everything.

Don't say "No!" too often. Save "No!" for important things. Instead, try to distract your child when he starts to do something dangerous or naughty. Play with him or give him a toy.

"Childproof" your house. Put anything dangerous or breakable out of a toddler's reach. Offer choices. Maybe he refuses to put his jacket on. Ask him if he'd rather wear his blue sweater. Be a good role model to show him how to behave.

Sometimes discipline may be necessary. Most experts think that spanking or hitting a child doesn't teach good behavior. It may make a child feel angry or bad about himself. And it teaches him that it's okay to hit people.

Some people prefer to use time-outs. Just make sure that your time-outs aren't too long. Five minutes is a long time to a three- and four-year-old. Ten minutes is long enough for a five- or six-year-old. More than that and the child forgets what he's doing there. If you use time-outs, make sure both the parents and the grandparents understand and abide by the time limits.

Pick a room for time-out that isn't too exciting a place. The laundry room or a hallway might be suitable. If you send a child to his toy-filled room, it probably won't feel like punishment. Of course, always make sure your child knows why he has time-out. After he's served his time, hug him and tell him you love him.

The Father

All the plans that work for couples work for you, too, except that you don't have a partner to rely on. As a single parent, you have to rely more on your parents. Still, you need to discuss with them what responsibilities are yours and what might be theirs.

If your parents work outside the home, you need to find day care for your baby. Check these places out yourself. It's the parent's job, although your mother might agree to help you. Support services such as the Department of Human Services (DHS) or your high school counseling office can suggest places. The DHS can help pay for some places.

Give as much time to your baby as possible. This is true both when your child is an infant and when he is old enough to be fun. You need to get to know your baby from the start, and that means diapering, feeding, and bathing. If you choose to let your parents take over the raising of your child, you will miss out on having special time together.

The Mother

You may have no one but your parents, but you can still decide what help you need from them. Who will take day-to-day care of the baby? If your mother does, will the baby still know you're its real mother? Who will buy the diapers? Who will change them in the night? Who will warm the bottles? Who will take the baby to the doctor?

Many schools these days offer special programs for teenage parents (usually mothers). The school provides day care for your baby so that you can finish school. Instead of paying them, you spend your free time in the center. Sometimes you can help out with feedings. Sometimes you can go to classes on parenting. This way, you can still feel like your baby's real mother while letting others help you.

Your parents know a lot about taking care of babies. Ask for their advice. You may be surprised to find out they're pretty smart. Talk to the school nurse or the nurses at the doctor's office. They can show you what a growing baby needs. And the biggest need, aside from food and warmth, is your love.

You and your parents need to have the same ideas on child care. What will you do when the baby cries? Change it? Feed it? Let it cry? Carry it around? Your baby needs security. That means it needs both of you to follow the same plan of action.

Check out books on infant care. Talk to the nurses. Trust your mother if you trust her judgment. And then decide how both of you will raise this child.

Chapter 4

Completing Your Education/Getting a Job

*J*ulie and Dan fell in love. Julie got pregnant, they got married, and they had a beautiful baby. They lived with his parents so that both Julie and Dan could finish high school. Which they did—with honors. Julie began working on a nursing degree, and Dan worked at a print shop to help with expenses. Now that Julie's a nurse, Dan's in business school. And the baby is in kindergarten, secure that she is loved and wanted.

The Couple

As a couple, you may have more choices. One of you can stay at home while the other either finishes school or gets a job.

But you'll have problems too. You need a lot of support to raise a baby and work (or go to school)

It is important for a teen parent to finish his or her education.

at the same time. That's often why teenage marriages fall apart. The couple don't have as much time to spend together. School has homework. Work has its time clock. And the baby has its own needs.

So the better your support system, the more likely you'll finish school, start that career, and stay married.

The Father/The Mother

Don't think it's less important for the mother to finish her education. As single parents, you both have to depend on yourselves. That's why it's important to be in the best financial shape. And in these days, to get a well-paying job, you need at least a high school diploma.

Caring for a baby doesn't have to stop you. Check out alternative high school programs. Most schools have special classes so that teenage parents can finish their degrees. Check with your high school. Or arrange to work toward your GED through night-school classes.

Look into Job Corps training or vocational training. Get in touch with a job counselor; look one up in the phone book. Or call the State Department of Education (in the phone book under Government). Even if you have a baby, you can—and should—finish your schooling. You can't live well on welfare, and your parents are not always going to be available to you. Besides, you'll feel better when you're supporting the two of you *yourself.*

Chapter 5

Friendships, Dates, and Another Baby

*H*annah was thrilled to be pregnant, even though she was only 15. By the time she turned 16, she was a mother.

But she no longer had anything in common with her friends. They still wanted to party all night, but Hannah had a baby to feed. No one wanted to spend much time with Hannah because she was always tending the baby.

"Can't you leave the kid with your mother?" Sue asked one night.

"Well, Mom works all day herself," Hannah said. Seeing that her friends were about to go without her, she said, "Let me check. Maybe Mom'll watch her."

An hour later, Hannah was out with her friends. They hauled out a six-pack. Hannah watched them drink; she took a few sips herself. But she didn't feel as carefree as they did. She didn't want to go back to feed the baby with beer on her breath.

Once you have a child, you may feel differently about what you do with your friends.

Soon her friends were well into the second six-pack. Everything was funny to them. Hannah left at that point. "I have a kid to go home to," she said.

The Couple

Relationships take a lot of work. So does raising a baby. You need time to take care of responsibilities (work, school, the baby) and time for each other. Where will all that time come from?

That's where parents can help out. If you give them time to themselves every so often, maybe they'll do the same for you. They can take the baby to the park so you and your partner can be alone together.

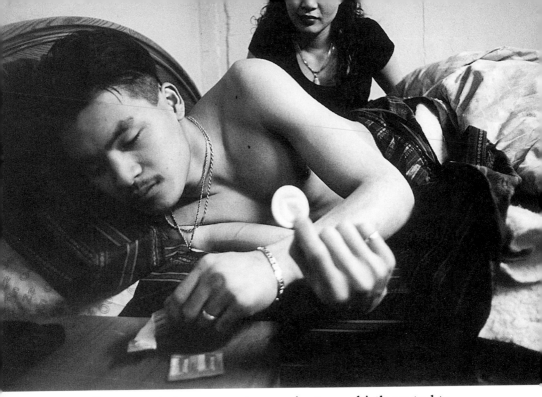

Even married teen parents are wise to use birth control to prevent unwanted pregnancy.

Be sure to set aside some private time for each of you. Even a bubble bath can calm your frazzled nerves. Or listening to music with headphones.

You'll both need your same-sex friends too. You'll probably find that they have changed (although it's really you who have changed). Still, you need to get out on your own, as long as you behave responsibly. That doesn't include getting drunk with your buddies!

As a couple, decide on a good form of birth control. Talk it over with a nurse or a counselor at a family planning center such as Planned Parenthood. Don't assume that you won't get pregnant again. It is important to be protected against unwanted pregnancy. You don't need another baby when your first one is still in diapers.

The best birth control devices are birth control pills, the diaphragm, and condoms, all used as directed. And don't forget that the condom is the only form of birth control that protects you from sexually transmitted diseases, including AIDS.

The Father

You're going to be pressed for time to go to school (or work), take care of a baby, hang out with the guys, and go out on a date. But you'll still want to do all those things.

If you're carrying your share of responsibility for the baby, your parents may offer to baby-sit so that you can go out on a date or with the guys. If they can't help you out, hire a baby-sitter. Teenage baby-sitters charge around five dollars an hour. Save some money, and get on with your personal life. It will be well worth it for an hour or two.

Just be sure that you can find a good baby-sitter, one who knows how to take care of an infant and who isn't more interested in talking on the phone.

As for dating, at what point do you tell your date about "the baby"? You don't need to announce your parenthood on the radio, but there's no point in hiding it, either. If it's just a date, who cares? If the relationship becomes more serious, she'll need to know sooner or later. Better sooner.

The only way to be completely certain of protecting yourself from pregnancy and sexually transmitted diseases (STDS) is by abstaining from sexual activity —not having sex. If you do decide to be sexually active, be careful. Always use a condom to protect yourself and your partner from pregnancy and STDS such as AIDS (which is always fatal). Make sure your partner is using birth control too. Don't assume. Ask and make sure.

But why be in such a hurry to have sex? Get to know women outside of a bedroom. Take your baby with you on dates sometimes. Your baby is part of your life now.

The Mother

You have a major new responsibility. But you're also entitled to go out and have fun once in a while. This might include doing things with friends or dating your baby's father or other men.

The only sure way to guard yourself against unwanted pregnancy and infection by any of the STDS is by not having sex at all. If you do decide to be sexually active, use birth control every time. Make certain your partner uses a condom to help protect you both from sexually transmitted diseases, including AIDS.

It's hard to date when you're taking care of a baby. Maybe you could take the baby with you on some dates. If the guy doesn't like kids, you might as well find out early. Maybe your parents will baby-sit once in a while. Maybe you could even

Despite your new responsibilities, you are entitled to treat yourself once in a while.

trade off with a friend who has a baby. You do need to have a life of your own. You need to be a person besides being a mother.

You may miss your old life. That's the hard part about being a teenage mother (or father, for that matter). You can't be like your old friends who don't have babies. You can't easily get into what they're doing, and they may not be interested in hearing about "the baby." Your friendships will change, but you don't have to give them up. Find new friends (other teen mothers) from support groups. Your family planning clinic can help. Your high school can help if it has a program for teen parents. You'll have more in common with your new friends, but remember some old buddies. Sometimes it's good to get away from baby talk and hear what's going on with the rest of the world.

One last thing. If you thought a baby might make your boyfriend marry you, remember that *it didn't work*. Don't think a second baby is sure to hook him. One of my friends ended up with two kids in a year's time. She was only seventeen. She thought her boyfriend would marry her if she had a boy the second time. It didn't work out that way . . .

Chapter 6

Setting Realistic Goals

In this section it doesn't matter whether you're a couple, a teen father, or a teen mother. You need to learn to depend on yourself. Your parents won't always be there. A marriage may fall apart, but you'll always have yourself.

To become self-reliant (which means to depend on yourself), you need three things:

- physical security (a safe environment)
- financial security (enough money to cover the bills)
- self-esteem (feeling good about yourself).

Physical Security

For most of you, living with your parents is a safe environment. But what if your parents abuse each other? Or hit you, or are rough with the

If there is abuse in your home, you should seek help for you and your baby.

baby? You can't stay in an abusive home without risking your baby's life as well as your own. Even though you're a teenager, you can still get help.

If you have no other place to go with your baby, call the crisis hotline for domestic violence. It's in the front of all phone books. Battered women (or women in danger of being beaten) can find temporary shelter. You don't have to be 18 or 21 to seek shelter. Any teen mother is considered an adult. The shelter will find temporary shelter for you and your baby.

Of course, finding an empty bed in a shelter these days is not easy. But once you're in, counselors will help you with housing, job counseling, and legal assistance. They'll give you a head start on getting out.

Even if your parents are fine, you never know how long you can live with them. Eventually, you will want to be on your own. You'll want your own space. You may feel more like an adult when you're no longer under your parents' roof.

Think about your baby's needs too. Would it be best to move to a cheap apartment so you all can have your privacy? Or would that be worse because the neighborhood is dangerous? Make sure you're not running from a bad situation to a worse one.

Agencies can help you become self-reliant. Check out the Department of Human Services and even your local mental health center.

Financial Security

Before you can move out on your own, you have to have money. That usually means getting a good job. If you haven't finished school, you should do that first. Get yourself in the best shape to land a variety of jobs. The more you can do, the more choices you'll have.

You can't have a safe, stable environment unless you have money coming in each week or month. Relying on welfare isn't the same as relying on a paycheck. It has to do with self-esteem. Most people don't feel right about things that are just handed to them. Without working, you won't have financial security. Without financial security, you won't have a safe environment. And without a safe environment, you won't feel good about yourself. They all go together.

When you get the job, you'll probably fill in a W-4 IRS form for your employer. Let's say you work thirty hours a week at minimum pay. No federal income tax payments should be withheld. Of course, other deductions will be taken out.

If you also file a federal income tax 1040 form the following year, you will collect about $2,200 in Earned Income Credit.

Your monthly budget (based on take-home earnings of $575 a month) might look like this:

- savings: $25/month (and
                                   Federal Earned
                                   Income Credit
                                   payment)
- room and board: $200/month
- baby's diapers, food: $240/month
- formula, clothing,
  supplies, medical,
  child-care,
  miscellaneous: $110/month
- your clothing, personal
  items, entertainment,
  gifts, or whatever
  comes up

You'll have a more positive outlook on parenting if you are able to provide for your baby.

Self-Esteem

The way to improve your self-esteem is to set goals for yourself. Taking care of yourself and your child is a fine goal, but it may be too big to start with. Besides, you need some support. If your parents can't provide you with support, look to other positive role models. We call them *mentors*. A mentor could be someone you admire who goes to your church, or someone you meet regularly at the library. It could be a favorite teacher, a social worker, or a garage mechanic. Get to know these people. How did they get where they are?

First, set some small goals for yourself, like getting your GED, or taking one class. Then set bigger goals. If you are not ready to work just yet, see if you can help out at the library storytime—and take your baby along. The important thing is to be *doing something positive.* If you plan for your future, you stand a better chance of making that future look good.

One last point: Once you've moved out, don't keep running home to your parents with problems. Try to handle them on your own, or seek professional help. Your folks don't need to know how many dates didn't work out, or how many times you thought your spouse was cheating on you. If you involve them in your life that way, you can't tell them to "mind your own business." You've just made *everything* their business.

Being an attentive and involved parent is a difficult but rewarding task.

Chapter 7

Understanding Your Growing Child

Even if you don't have a lot of money or you haven't yet finished your education, you can still provide your child with what he or she needs most: love.

It's important to play with your child. Give him or her toys and a safe place to explore. And talk to him or her all the time. Babies and toddlers like the sound of your voice.

Routines are important to a baby and especially to a toddler. It makes him or her feel that life is safe. Set naps at the same time each day, meals at the same time, bedtime at the same time.

Read to your child. Kids love stories, and they love having you close to them. It also helps you keep up your reading skills. If you can't always read to your child, borrow some tapes from the library and let your child listen to them on his or her own.

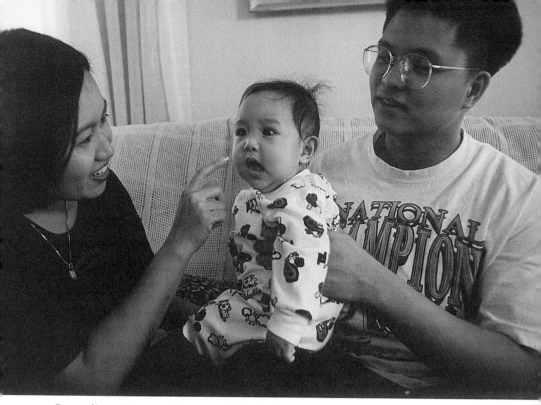

Spending time with your baby is important to the child's development.

You don't have to buy your child expensive toys. Kids love boxes at first more than what's inside them. Bring home groceries in a box and save the box for your toddler. Make blocks out of empty half-gallon milk cartons. Let your toddler play on the floor with your pots and pans and some wooden spoons.

Your growing child will be able to work his larger muscles before his smaller ones. He'll be able to run and climb better than cut with scissors and use crayons. Give your child a chance to try out all kinds of things. Just be sure to supervise. A toddler can be fearless and quick. He could be out in the street before you know it.

Even though you're a teenager, you are still the parent. Get involved with your child. If she's in day care, make sure it's a safe place. Drop in at different times to see if your child is being taken care of. Don't go overboard, though, demanding that your child have most of the attention. Be protective, but be realistic too.

If you're a father raising a daughter, or a mother raising a son, it's a good idea to have good role models of the opposite sex. Down the road, it'll help your little girl or boy to have both men and women friends.

Finally, whether you live with your parents or not, be sure to behave yourself in front of the child. Kids understand more than you think. They know when everyone's angry. It's okay for them to see that people get angry, as long as those people don't act out their anger.

If you swear in front of your child, you'll be sorry when he swears at the minister the next time you're in church. If you say bad things about your partner, or men in general, your son will understand that you think all males (including him) are bad. The same is true for trashing women to your daughter. Kids watch how their parents (married or not) treat each other. And that's how they learn.

Realize that your growing child will want independence, just as you probably do from your own parents. Toddlers are known for pitching fits,

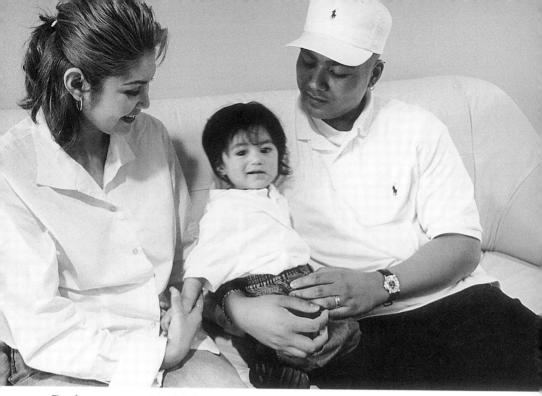

Both parents should be a part of their child's life.

throwing food around, and pulling off their clothes,
just to show that they can do it. Don't take it too
seriously. They're trying to become "self-reliant,"
and that's something we all need to do.

If you find that you are overwhelmed, or if you are
afraid that you might hurt your baby out of anger
or frustration, there are people who can help.
Parents Anonymous helps parents learn effective
and healthy ways to handle their children. Their
number is listed on page 61. You don't have to be
ashamed; just find the help that you need for you
and your baby.

Give your children supervision and plenty of love.
With luck, that is what your parents gave you during your first years.

Appendix

Advice from Teenage Parents Living at Home

What do you NOT like about living at home with your baby and your parents?

"My dad giving me information that I already have."

"I think maybe they help me too much, and when I move out, I won't know what to do. I think I should be an adult, and when I live with my parents, they tell me what to do."

"They always tell me how to raise my kid. They tell me what to do, when to do it and how to do it. It's like he [the baby] is their kid and I'm the nanny."

"Living at home with my parents is hard because I am the baby of the family, and everyone wants to tell me how to take care of my son."

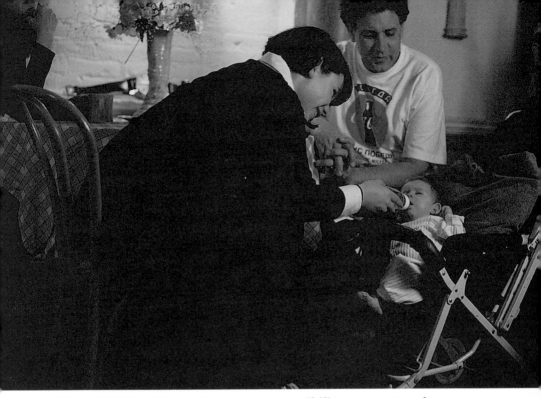

Your child is ultimately your responsibility, no matter how much your parents help you out.

"My mother and I always argue because we don't have enough money to buy me a car so I can get to school and home along with my baby to and from day care. We also argue because I spend too much money."

"The only thing I don't like is my parents trying to tell me how to raise my six-month-old daughter."

"Well, I don't like my father, so that's a bad thing plus I'd rather it just be my baby and me."

"My mom thinks she knows everything. She expects me to give my son to her so she can take better care of him."

"What I don't like is the fact that my mother gives her [the baby] things that I wouldn't want her to have. My mother always pushes me about money, but when I work a lot, she gripes that I never see my child."

"I still get treated like a child sometimes. My parents go against my wishes when it comes to my baby, and they try to tell me how to raise her. They try to take over and tell me what to do."

"My parents are always on my case, and they tell me how much of a burden my son and I are. They put my son's father down and always harass me about getting a job."

What are GOOD things about living at home with your baby and your parents?

"They stay out of my way and let me raise him the way I want."

"They help me a lot both financially and emotionally. They give me breaks when I am frustrated."

"I like that she [my baby] has love from all around, and that I have help with her."

"My mom is just trying to help. She feeds me and helps me with my son."

"If you're not sure about something, you can ask them because they have more experience. And when I'm sick, my mom helps me."

"I have some help in the middle of the night."

"My mom gives me a break when I am frustrated or when I want to go out."

"Living at home helps. I don't have to pay rent. I can get my son on my dad's insurance, which means doctor visits only cost $10 each time. My mom helps me out when I get frustrated or I need to get sleep for school, or laundry needs to be done."

"They help me out with buying everything, and if I need a baby-sitter, they're almost always available. On the weekends they wake up with him [the baby] and let me sleep in."

"They are always there to baby-sit him when I work or go out. They give me advice. It's good because I don't have to pay bills or rent. I don't make much money, and I'd be poor if I had to support my kid and pay bills, too."

"My dad helps me with the baby."

Glossary—*Explaining New Words*

abortion   Intentional ending of a pregnancy.

adoption   Taking as one's own the child of other parents.

approval   Acceptance of a person or situation.

environment   The surroundings in which a person finds himself; the combination of surrounding physical factors such as climate.

maturity   The quality of having completed one's natural development.

personal space   The immediate environment in which one lives without feeling crowded by other people or things.

responsibility   Accountability for a situation or a set of circumstances; reliability.

routine   Established order of events such as to provide regularity.

security   State of being free from danger or fear.

supportive   Acting to provide help or assistance or to defend another's rights.

vocational training   Education or specialized training leading to a particular skill or job.

Where to Go for Help

If you are pregnant and need counseling, talk to a teacher, guidance counselor, doctor, family friend, clergy member, or another adult you trust. To find help in your local community, call the Legal Aid Society, Parents Without Partners, Planned Parenthood, Salvation Army, or United Way.

For help with child abuse, contact your local Children's Aid Society or police department.

National Committee to
   Prevent Child Abuse
332 S. Michigan Avenue
Suite 1600
Chicago, IL 60604
(800) CHILDREN (phone)
(312) 939-8962 (fax)
Web site with parenting tips:
   http://www.childabuse.org/

National Youth Crisis Hotline
(800) 448-4663

Parents Without Partners
(800) 637-7974

Pampers Parenting
   Institute—Total Baby Care
http://www.pampers.com/

Planned Parenthood
   Federation of America

810 Seventh Avenue
New York, NY 10019
(212) 541-7800 (phone)
(800) 230-PLAN (appointments)
(212) 245-1845 (fax)
e-mail: communications@
   ppfa.org
Web site: http://www.planned
   parenthood.org/

Positive Parenting Online
Web site: http://www.positive
   parenting.com/

In Canada

Planned Parenthood
   Federation of Canada
1 Nicholas Street, Suite 430
Ottawa, ON K1N 7B7
(613) 241-4474
Web site: http://www.ppfc.ca

For Further Reading

Ayer, Eleanor H. *Everything You Need to Know About Teen Fatherhood*. Rev. ed. New York: Rosen Publishing Group, 1995.

Green, Martin I. *A Sigh of Relief*. New York: Bantam Books, 1994.

Hammerslough, Jane. *Everything You Need to Know About Teen Motherhood*. Rev. ed. New York: Rosen Publishing Group, 1997.

Kandel, Bethany, with Thelma Kandel. *The Expert Parent: Everything You Need to Know from All the Experts in the Know*. New York: Pocket Books, 1997.

Lindsay, Jeanne Warren. *Teen Dads: Rights, Responsibilities and Joys*. Buena Park, Calif.: Morning Glory Press, 1993

Lindsay, Jeanne Warren, and Sally McCullough. *Teens Parenting: Discipline from Birth to Three*. Buena Park, Calif.: Morning Glory Press, 1991.

Lindsay, Jeanne Warren and Jean Brunelli, PHN. *Teens Parenting: Your Pregnancy and Newborn Journey*. Buena Park, California: Morning Glory Press, 1991.

Trapani, Margi. *Listen Up! Teenage Mothers Speak Out*. New York: Rosen Publishing Group, Inc., 1997.

Trapani, Margi. *Reality Check: Teenage Fathers Speak Out*. New York: Rosen Publishing Group, Inc. 1997.

Index

Acknowledgments
Special thanks to Jo Ann Bierig of the Margaret Hudson School in Broken
Arrow, Oklahoma, and her teenage student-parents for their advice on this
book.
    Thanks, too, to Georgie Rasco of the Oklahoma Coalition Against
Domestic Violence and Sexual Assault.

About the Author
Carolyn Simpson teaches psychology at Tulsa Junior College, Tulsa,
Oklahoma. She has been a social worker and has taught in a school for teen
parents in Bridgton, Maine. She and her husband have three kids of their
own.

Photo Credits
Cover photo, p. 57 by Michael Brandt; pp. 12, 15, 39 by Katherine Hsu; pp.
25, 28, 43 by Kim Sonsky; all other photos by Yung-Hee Chia.